PHILOSOPHY OF RELIGION 1

RELIGIOUS LANGUAGE

BY
PETER COLE
AND
JOHN LEE

© Copyright 1994
First published 1994
Reprinted 2007

Abacus Educational Services,
20 Malvern Close
Worthing,
West Sussex
BN11 2HE.

ISBN 1 898653 05 4

Other titles available in the series:

Also available:

Ethics series:

Other titles on the Fourth Gospel are also available.

CONTENTS

INTRODUCTION

This series of booklets has been written specifically to cater for the needs of A/AS students of Religious Studies. However it may equally be used as an introduction to the philosophy of religion by the interested lay person or by first year undergraduates.

The style of this booklet is similar to the booklets in the Synoptic Gospels series and the Fourth Gospel series. It is structured around a series of key questions which have developed from classroom experience. It also contains a section that deals with misunderstandings that frequently arise and is useful for both teaching and revision.

Further booklets in this series are being produced.

WHAT IS THE PROBLEM WITH RELIGIOUS LANGUAGE?

People use words. Many words are used to talk about religion. Indeed religions and religious believers may use language in a variety of different ways. Language could, for example, be used by a religious believer in order to show that she/he is committed to a religion. Further, language could be used to promote different types of behaviour or be used to worship a deity. This type of language can often be poetic (consider, for example, hymns). In addition, there are a number of words that are specific to religion - such as "Holy". However, there is another way in which religious language is used and that is to make assertions i.e. try to say something about how things are. Someone could, for example, make the claim (i.e. assert) that we will be reincarnated after death.

It is this idea of assertions that philosophers of religion are often interested in and it is with assertions that many philosophers feel that there are problems. For example, someone could claim that "God is good". The problem with this is, according to some, that it might not be clear what this actually means. Most people know what the words "God" and "good" mean but there is a problem: the word "good" is used to refer to human activities. Can it be applied to God? Would it mean the same?

Take another example: God is timeless. The difficulty with this statement is that it is not possible to explain the word "timeless". Everything we experience happens in time and it is difficult to understand something that is not in time.

The heart of the problem seems to be that religious assertions attempt to refer to things beyond anyone's experience. They describe the "infinite", the "mysterious" and other metaphysical ideas that are not dealt with by our everyday language and it is thus difficult to see whether these religious terms have meaning.

DOES THIS IMPLY THAT RELIGIOUS LANGUAGE IS MEANINGLESS?

Many philosophers have felt that in order to discuss whether religious language is meaningless (or meaningful) it is important to determine some criterion of meaning i.e. some rule by which words can be judged either "meaningful" or "meaningless". In the 1920's and 1930's many philosophers dedicated a lot of discussion to such a question. (The question may be put as "what is the meaning of 'meaning'?") One group of such philosophers was based in Vienna and has become known as the "Vienna Circle". The Vienna Circle included such philosophers as Schlick and Carnap.

However, some of the ideas that the Vienna Circle adopted can be traced back to an 18th Century Scottish philosopher David Hume. Hume believed that all our ideas are based on sensations (experiences); for example we have an idea of "trees" because we have experienced (come across) many of them. Hume also believed that this is where true knowledge comes from: we need to have experienced something in order to know it. In other words any idea we have, however complex, can be reduced to some experience that our senses have provided. Hume called this knowledge "matters of fact".

However, Hume recognized that there do seem to be other types of knowledge, such as logic and mathematics, which do not seem to be based on experience; but Hume argued that such "knowledge" is merely based on the "relation of ideas" and tells us nothing about the world itself. (Hume's view is usually known as "Empiricism".)

It is this distinction between "matters of fact" and the "relation of ideas" that is central to the work of the Vienna Circle. Accepting that knowledge is based on experience, they felt that this could also be applied to language; a criterion of meaning could be established. As Hume had argued that knowledge is based on experience, the Vienna Circle felt that experience is the key to determining whether a sentence is meaningful or not.

6

The criterion of meaning that the Vienna Circle thus developed asserted that a sentence could only be meaningful if some sense experience could count in its favour. In other words it had to be verifiable i.e. we could actually see, hear or touch it in order to discover whether it was true or false. Thus a sentence must be considered meaningless if it could not be verified. This theory has become known as the Verification Principle.

Similar to Hume, the principle also allows for the fact that some sentences may be meaningful not because they are verifiable but by virtue of the words involved; for example, "a spinster is an unmarried woman" is meaningful (and true) because spinster means "unmarried woman". However, it was argued that such statements are "trivial" because they tell us nothing about the actual world.

The Verification Principle was only part of the work of the Vienna Circle and it was adopted by other philosophers. Indeed the members of the Vienna Circle are more widely known as "logical positivists" and their theories as "logical positivism".

Underlying the ideas of a "Verification Principle" and logical positivism is the belief that philosophy (and the methods that philosophy uses) should be similar to science since science, by the use of experiments and observations, had proved successful in that it had resulted in agreed knowledge. Coupled with this was the belief that metaphysics (that which talks about the ultimate and that science cannot answer) was fruitless.

So what sentences have to be considered meaningless, if the Verification Principle is accepted? Clearly most religious assertions could not be accepted because they refer to things beyond experience and thus cannot be verified by sense experience. Even if, for example, it was claimed that God can be experienced through His use of miracles, this would still have to be rejected as meaningless since it is not God's intervention that is experienced by the senses rather it is the (supposed) effect that this has. Thus it was felt that religious language must be meaningless.

However, the principle, by its very nature, also rules as meaningless many statements that most believe are meaningful. For example, there is no experiment that could verify the truth of historical statements such as "Christopher Columbus arrived in America in 1492"; but clearly most people would argue that this is a meaningful statement (and indeed true). Similarly scientific statements, such as "all metals expand when it is heated", would also have to be considered meaningless since it is not possible to observe (and therefore verify) every piece of metal every time it is heated and therefore we cannot state that *all* metal expands when it is heated.

It was considerations such as these that led many philosophers to shy away from such a strict application of the Verification Principle. (Although some members of the Vienna Circle, e.g. Schlick, argued that such things as scientific laws were meaningless: they were nonsense but "useful nonsense".) One philosopher who attempted to reinterpret the Verification Principle is A.J. Ayer. Although Ayer was not actually a member of the Vienna Circle his book, *Language, Truth and Logic*, is probably the most famous defence of logical positivism. In this book Ayer outlines a distinction between verifiability "in principle" and verifiability "in practice". It is obviously not possible, he argues, that scientific laws could be verified in practice, but they could in theory: we know what it would take to observe every piece of metal. However, even this is not possible for religious statements as we do not even know in principle what sense experience would count in their favour.

Further, Ayer introduces another distinction between what he calls "strong verification" and "weak verification". The distinction is based on the two different ideas of the word verify. The first is taking verify to mean "observe" and the second is "have some sense-experience that counts towards". This is perhaps best explained with an example: the theory that there are atoms. Atoms cannot be observed as such, so the theory is meaningless according to the "strong" version of verification. However, it is possible to construct some experiments to suggest the existence of atoms: this is what is meant by "weak verification"; and it is this "weak" form that Ayer argues is correct.

▶ CRITICISMS.

(i) Should religious statements, therefore, be considered meaningless? The Verification Principle should give no reason to believe this;

indeed it is probably one of the most discredited theories of the 20th century. In 1978 Ayer himself admitted that his earlier work was "mostly false".

At the heart of any criticism of the Verification Principle is the idea that the theory itself does not make much sense. For example, suppose we want to determine whether statement X is true. Using the Verification Principle we need to see whether statement X is verifiable. How are we going to go about this? Surely we need to know what statement X means before we can decide whether it is verifiable or not. In other words when we look at any statement we need to make a judgement about it (i.e. understand it) before we decide how we can verify it. Suppose we looked at "this jumper is black". I could observe that this was both a jumper and black but only because I know what both these words mean.

(ii) Further, why should we accept the meaningfulness of the Verification Principle itself? There is no sense experience that could count in its favour: the theory itself is not verifiable. Thus if we accepted the theory, we would have to argue that the theory itself is meaningless.

(iii) Indeed it does not even seem that the Verification Principle actually rules out religious language. Some philosophers such as John Hick argue that religious statements could be verified by what he calls an "eschatological verification". God's existence, for example, could be verified by each of us after we die. Hick illustrates his point by the story of two people travelling down a road. One believes that the road leads to a Celestial City but the other doesn't. The only way they'll find out who's right is when they get to the end of the road.

(iv) Further, if we were to accept a "weak" form of verification there does appear to be some evidence for some religious statements; it could be argued that the beauty of the world suggests that it has a creator. In addition some religious claims are historical ones (for example "Jesus rose from the dead") and are therefore not ruled out by the weak form of verification.

COULD THERE BE ANOTHER CRITERION OF MEANING?

As has been said, many of the conclusions of logical positivism were based on the idea that philosophy should model itself on science. Science was seen by the logical positivists as being concerned with the collection of information and the subsequent development of theories. For example, a scientist might observe that whenever a piece of metal is heated it expands and, after making further observations, might conclude that all metal expands when it is heated. However, this view of science has been challenged. Karl Popper, for example, argued that science did not move from observation to theory but rather from theory to observation. In other words theories are considered true until some evidence counts against them i.e. are *falsified*.

It is this idea of falsification that some philosophers believed could be the basis for developing a different criterion of meaning. As well as applying falsification as a test for the truth of scientific theories, it was thought that it could also be applied to test the meaningfulness of statements. Scientific theories were only considered true as long as they were not falsified. However, even though no evidence has counted against any scientific theory that is considered true, the theory is still meaningful because we know what evidence would disprove it i.e. what set of circumstances would falsify it. But what of statements that no observation could ever count against? It was these sort of statements that some philosophers thought should be considered meaningless. In other words if a statement asserts nothing, then it cannot mean anything.

One philosopher who adopted this idea of falsification was Antony Flew. He illustrated the idea by means of a parable:

> Once upon a time two explorers came across a clearing in the jungle. In the clearing were growing many flowers and many weeds. One explorer says, "Some gardener must tend this plot." The other disagrees... So they pitch their tents and set a watch. No gardener is ever seen. "But perhaps he is an invisible

gardener." So ...they patrol with bloodhounds ...(but) the blood-hounds never give cry. Yet still the Believer is not convinced. "But there is a gardener, invisible, intangible, ...a gardener who has no scent and makes no sound." At last the Sceptic despairs, "But what remains of your original assertion? Just how does what you call an invisible, intangible, eternally elusive gardener differ from an imaginary gardener or even from no gardener at all?" (from "Theology and Falsification", in *New Essays in Philosophical Theology* ed. Flew and MacIntyre 1955)

It is clear that the parable is being used by Flew to suggest that religious statements can have no meaning. In the parable the Believer does not allow anything to count against the idea that there is a gardener. Similarly, Flew argued, the religious believer allows nothing to count against religious statements. Religious statements, therefore, cannot be falsified and are thus meaningless.

▶CRITICISMS.

(i) Flew's idea of falsification led to a series of articles that responded to his conclusions. Known as the "University Debate", these articles were written between 1950 and 1951 and were published in a journal entitled "University". Two critics of Flew were R.M. Hare and Basil Mitchell.

(a) Hare.

Hare accepted Flew's idea that falsification could be used to determine the meaningfulness of statements. However, he argued that falsification did not apply to religious statements. Hare suggested that when Flew looked at religious statements he was taking them to be factual statements that could either be true of false i.e. assertions. However, Hare did not consider religious statements to be factual ones. He argued that although nothing can count against religious statements (i.e. they are not falsifiable) this did not imply that they had to be meaningless, rather religious statements must be something other than assertions. In other words religious language could not make factual claims.

However, Hare believed that religious statements could still have some sort of meaning. The "meaning" of religious statements is not, according to Hare, to impart knowledge about the world, rather meaning arises from the way that religious statements are used and the impact that they have on people's lives. Hare coined the word "blik" to help explain his point. A "blik" is a particular way of looking at the world and if someone adopts some sort of blik she/he may interpret her/his experiences differently.

Hare illustrated his idea of "bliks" by a story of a lunatic who is convinced that all university dons want to kill him. The lunatic is introduced to numerous kindly dons but is still convinced that they want to kill him; he claims that their kindliness is a ploy to lure him off his guard. In this example the lunatic has adopted a "blik" and this affects the way that he looks at all the evidence presented to him. His claim that all university dons want to kill him is not falsifiable, but it does have an impact on the way that he views things and therefore does have some meaning. Religious statements are, according to Hare, like bliks (ways of looking at the world) and they are therefore meaningful because thy have significance for the people using them.

(b) Mitchell.

Basil Mitchell attacked Flew's ideas for different reasons. Mitchell argued that there is in fact evidence that counts against religious claims and that many religious believers are aware of this. As an example Mitchell used the "Problem of Evil". [Why doesn't an all-powerful, all-loving God remove evil?] Mitchell argued that clearly the believer would take this as evidence against the existence of an all-loving God. Religious statements are therefore not meaningless because evidence does count against them. However, Mitchell points out that many believers may not reject their religious ideas even when presented with evidence against them. The reason for this is that the believer has a bias against dropping his/her belief and will therefore not change it in the face of evidence; but this does not mean that the believer does not recognize that there is evidence against his/her beliefs or that the believer will always remain a believer. (This is what might be called "faith".)

Mitchell illustrated his idea with the tale of a Freedom Fighter. We witness the actions of this Freedom Fighter but sometimes some of the things that he does do not appear to be in our favour. (He might, for example, blow up bridges in our way.) However, we still believe that the Freedom Fighter is on our side: we do not take the things that he does as evidence that he is against us, rather we trust that he has an overall plan that is working for our good.

(ii) Both Hare and Mitchell when responding to the idea of falsification accepted, to a certain extent, that it could be used as a criterion for determining meaning. However, there do seem to be problems with the Falsification Principle itself. Many have argued that statements can have meaning even if they cannot be falsified. Richard Swinburne, for example, illustrated this idea with the story about "Toys in the Cupboard". These toys only come out and move around when nobody is watching them. In other words the fact that these toys come out could never be falsified. However, Swinburne argues that it is clear that we understand the idea of these toys coming out: the claim is meaningful and this shows that the falsification principle cannot work.

IS THERE A WAY OF SOLVING THE PROBLEM OF RELIGIOUS LANGUAGE?

It is now generally agreed that the ideas of "verification" and "falsification" do not provide a criterion for establishing meaning. However, it may still not be clear as to how we could talk about religious ideas. Our initial problem that religious language refers to things beyond our experience remains. In the history of philosophy there have been two main approaches as to how religious ideas (especially God) might be talked about.

▶ (i) NEGATION.

Some have argued that even though it may not be possible to describe God, it is possible to say what He is not. For example, it could be said that "God is not evil" and, joined with many other similar statements, this can actually tell us something about God.

However, others have argued that this idea of "negation" cannot really tell us anything about God since saying what He is not, never pinpoints exactly what He is.

▶ (ii) ANALOGY.

Another way in which some philosophers have felt that it is possible to talk about God is through analogy. An analogy is a comparison of two (or more) different things that points out the ways in which they are similar. For instance, a writer may explain a new idea by comparing it to more familiar experiences. A famous example of an analogy is William Paley's comparison of the universe and a watch.

(a) Aquinas.

In the thirteenth century Thomas Aquinas used the idea of analogy to try and show that it is possible to talk about God. Aquinas first looked at the way the same word may be used to describe different things. (For example the word "good" may be used to describe both a book and a dog.) Aquinas said that a word could be used in two

14

ways: either univocally when it is used to mean exactly the same thing; or equivocally when it is used in a completely different way. However, Aquinas argued that when we talk about God we cannot use words either univocally or equivocally rather we must appeal to the idea of analogy and say that the words are used in a similar, though not identical, way.

Aquinas' idea that we can talk about God through analogy has been criticized. For an analogy to be valid there needs to be some basis of comparison. If God is meant to be entirely different from human concepts, it is difficult to see how an analogy could be made. Aquinas did seem to be aware of this problem. He argued that there is a relationship between the world and God (for example He created and sustains the world) and therefore there is a point of comparison. Indeed Aquinas felt that there are two ways in which analogies can be used to talk about God: proportion and attribution. For example, we can understand "God is omnipotent" by using an analogy of proportion. We have a human idea of what it means to be able to do something and this can be used as our basis for understanding God. God, however, is proportionally more powerful than humans so although we cannot completely understand the idea of omnipotence we can have an insight into it. Aquinas' idea of attribution is based on the idea that many human characteristics are derived from God's. For example, Aquinas saw human wisdom as a reflection of God's.

(b) Ramsey.

A twentieth century development of this idea of analogy can be seen in the work of Ian Ramsey and is perhaps best expressed in his book *Religious Language*. Ramsey had two key terms that he used when he talked about religious language: "models" and "qualifiers". A model is something that represents something else and helps us understand the original. With respect to religious language our understanding of particular words is, according to Ramsey, the model of our understanding of God. For example, we all have some understanding of the word "good" and this can provide a model for understanding God. However, if we want to understand God we need to adapt our model - we need to qualify it. So to say that "God is good" we need to add the qualifier that He is *infinitely* good. The effect of this qualifier, according to Ramsey, will lead us on to thinking about God's goodness in greater and greater depth. Eventually the "penny will drop" and we will gain an insight into "infinite goodness"; we cannot express this insight (which Ramsey calls a disclosure) but it has been evoked by the qualifier. Ramsey also believed that when we gain this insight we will respond to it: it will create a sense of wonder and a sense of commitment.

IS RELIGIOUS LANGUAGE SYMBOLIC?

As has been seen Aquinas believed that it was possible to talk about God through analogy and Ramsey developed this approach. Underlying their ideas is that something can represent something else. Many philosophers and theologians have used this idea when discussing religious language. In other words they think that it is possible to say something meaningful about God even though what they are saying may not be literal. This approach sees religious language as symbolic.

There are a number of ways in which religious language may be used in this non-literal way.

(i) SIMILE.

A simile is a statement in which something is described as being similar to something else. A simile is a way of making an analogy that uses symbolic language. For example, "the kingdom of God is like a mustard seed" is a simile. The mustard seed is not meant literally, rather it is symbolic.

(ii) METAPHOR.

An extension of this idea of simile is a metaphor. Metaphors are widely used in religion. A metaphor, like a simile, is a comparison even though it appears not to be one (This is because, in a metaphor, words such as "like" are not used.) For example, "the Lord is my shepherd" is a metaphor.

Traditionally metaphors have been seen as another way of saying what could be said literally. However, some have questioned this view and see metaphors as expressing something which could not be expressed directly. Metaphors are seen to be a way in which we talk about the unfamiliar.

(iii) SIGNS.

Signs are perhaps the most common form of symbolic language

and are used to represent a specific object, person or event. Signs are often used as a convenient shorthand way of communicating and usually the meaning of the sign has to be learnt. Road signs are a very good example. For instance, a driver may come across a circular white road-sign with a diagonal black line across it. Unless the driver has learnt what this sign means its meaning would not be obvious. (It informs the driver that the national speed limit applies.)

Some signs have become universal whilst others have different meanings within different cultures. For instance, in the West white is a sign of purity whereas in the East it is a sign for death. Some signs have a logical connection with what they represent e.g. the sign of the fish as used in Christianity. Some signs have the power to evoke feelings such as, for some people, their national flag. Within religions there are a number of different signs that might be examined. However, in religions it is symbols that tend to be more common.

(iv) SYMBOLS.

A symbol, like a sign, is a form of language and stands for something other than itself. Whereas signs can be arbitrary and bear no obvious relationship to what they represent, a symbol has been derived from experience. Signs denote things which are already understood, whereas symbols use everyday images but use them to direct our way of thinking and to speak of the transcendent. There are many religious symbols and images such as light, darkness and water which are found in all religions. They are common attempts to understand and express the meaning of the universe.

Religions, therefore, use symbols as one way of communicating. However, some have argued that even religious language that does not appear to be symbolic is actually symbolic. In other words the traditional understanding of God (and other religious ideas) needs to be reinterpreted. One proponent of such a view was Paul Tillich (see, for example, *The Shaking of the Foundations*). Tillich argued that our idea of God needs retranslation. He defines God not as an external being but as "that which concerns us ultimately" or the "ground of our being". Therefore, for Tillich, when we talk about God we are not talking about a being but about "being itself".

18

(v) MYTHS.

A myth is a story. For many people to refer to a story as a "myth" is to imply that the story is untrue as it does not correspond to our modern scientific ideas. However, some have argued that, although not literally true, myths can still have meaning. They are attempts to state some eternal truth in terms of an earthly picture i.e. they are symbolic. Myths are not seen as historical records but as stories that provide insights about our own existence.

Probably the most well known person who examined myths was Bultmann. Bultmann was a theologian who argued that the world view presented in the New Testament (i.e. one that is based on the supernatural) needs to be reinterpreted so that it is consistent with our modern world view. This process of reinterpretation he called "demythologization". What remains, according to Bultmanr, are the eternal truths contained in the myths of the New Testament.

▶PROBLEMS.

Two main issues arise if religious language is viewed as symbolic:

(i) Adequate and Appropriate?

The idea underpinning symbolic language is that something can represent something else. Religious symbols are about the ultimate and it seems difficult to decide whether a symbol can successfully represent that which is beyond our experience. There seems to be no way to judge whether a symbol is adequate i.e. does what it sets out to do. In addition there may be no way of determining whether a symbol gives the wrong insights about the ultimate i.e. is inappropriate. There has been much debate, for example, concerning whether "God is mother" is appropriate.

(ii) Realism?

The implication of the ideas of people such as Tillich is that religious language does not refer to something that has an objective reality. There is a strong tension between Tillich's ideas and the more traditional view (often known as "realism") that believes that statements can be and are about the objective world.

IS THERE A DIFFERENT WAY OF LOOKING AT LANGUAGE?

We have already considered a number of ways in which philosophers have tried to say what gives something meaning. For example, the logical positivists argued that meaning is the "method of verification". At the heart of many definitions of meaning is the belief that meaning can be determined by referring one thing to another. A common form of this idea is often expressed in terms of "pictures". Through sense experience we all have certain mental images or "pictures" of objects in the world and language is based on these mental images; a sentence is meaningful because it corresponds correctly to my mental images. For example, I understand the word "table" because I have attached this word to my mental picture of a table. In essence language has been seen, by some philosophers, as a way in which people label objects in the world. Indeed some philosophers have gone as far as saying that all words we use must be based ultimately on some sort of "picture" and hence this idea has become known as the "picture theory of meaning".

However, other philosophers have felt that language is more than just a process by which we label things: language has many different uses and functions. One of these uses of language is to perform something. I could, for example, say "shut the door" and this would be a command for you to do something. Similarly I could say "I promise to give you £10". The phrase "I promise" does not describe a fact, rather it performs a function and it creates a new situation. In other words language does not just describe objects it can be used to do things. This sort of language is known as performative language. As performative language does not describe facts it cannot be "true" or "false" rather it can only be used correctly or incorrectly. (It does not make sense to say, for example, that my command to you to "shut the door" could be false; I could, however, use it incorrectly, if, for instance there was no door in this room.)

This idea of performative language should already be familiar as Hare's idea of "bliks" is one way in which it has been applied to religious language. (See page 11) Another philosopher who used this idea was R.B, Braithwaite. Braithwaite argued that religious language is not trying to express knowledge, rather it is used by individuals and communities to perform different functions. Religious language is not a series of facts about the world, rather it is a way in which people say what they intend to do. Similar to many ideas that were considered in the previous section, Braithwaite argued that religious language is like a story: it is not literally true but it is used to inspire and guide behaviour i.e. it has practical value.

▶WITTGENSTEIN AND LANGUAGE GAMES.

Many of the ideas that have already been discussed are based, in part, on the work of the influential philosopher Ludwig Wittgenstein. Early on in his philosophical career Wittgenstein put forward a "picture theory of meaning" (like the one described above) but later on he re-examined the question of meaning and came to a different conclusion. He argued that it is unrealistic to suppose that all words are ultimately based on pictures and pointed out the fact that language is used in a variety of different ways. His ideas can be found in his *Philosophical Investigations.*

Wittgenstein likens language to a game that we play. There are many different games (e.g. chess, netball etc) each of which have their own rules. However, it does not make sense to take the rules of one game and apply them to another. (We could not, for example, play chess by passing a ball to each other.) Similarly language is used by many different people in many different contexts. Indeed it might be said that there are a number of different "language games" going on. The meaning of a word in one particular "game" is determined by the "rules" of that game i.e. it is determined by the way the word is used in that game. Therefore for Wittgenstein meaning is "use" rather than any sort of shared mental image.

At the heart of Wittgenstein's concept of "language games" is the idea that words only have meaning because of their context and therefore we have to be careful to know which "game" we are playing. For example, the word "castling" has no meaning if we are playing netball. Wittgenstein then applies this idea to philosophy and concludes that philosophical problems about language are created by not understanding that words can be used in different language games. Wittgenstein gives the example of the problems associated with the word "soul" and argues that these problems are caused by trying to see the soul as some sort of physical object. The problems, according to Wittgenstein, would be dissolved if it were realized that the "physical object" game simply does not apply to the soul.

How, therefore, do Wittgenstein's ideas apply to religious language? Firstly, if Wittgenstein's philosophy is adopted, the only way that the religious language game could be understood is by actually playing it. In other words what is needed is an "insider's" view so that religious terms can be put in their proper contexts. For example, the question "Was Jesus God?" cannot be given a yes/no answer; rather it depends on which game you are in when you ask the question. (A Jew and a Christian might give different but equally valid answers.) This implies that religious language could not be criticized by someone outside the game as she/he would be making the mistake of judging one game by the rules of another. Further, when religious language is discussed we are no longer interested in testing whether religious claims are true, rather we are interested in how religious words are used i.e. what function they have. This function could be to promote particular behaviour (see the ideas of Braithwaite above).

However, this view of religious language has been criticized. A question arises as to whether a religious language game is independent of other language games. The philosopher D.Z. Phillips, for example, argued that it was since it contains its own rules as to whether statements are "meaningful" or "true" and it cannot therefore be criticized by people playing different games. It is possible, however, to question this view as religious believers are aware of many different beliefs and do themselves play other language games. In other words it is difficult to see how the religious language game could be totally isolated from any other.

Further, there may be other problems with Wittgenstein's approach. As has already been explained it no longer makes sense for two people playing different games to discuss questions such as "Does God exist?" as the answer cannot be given in terms of "true" or "false"; rather the word "God" can only be used either correctly or incorrectly in a language game. (This view is often known as "conceptual relativism".) For many people this view leads to a contradiction as the question can be answered both "yes" and "no". Similarly many feel that such questions can be answered i.e. there is truth that is not entirely dependent on the context. Indeed many religious claims are claims that are believed to be true for everyone. For example, the claim in Christianity that Jesus died in order to bring salvation.

IS THERE A DIFFERENT WAY OF LOOKING AT RELIGION?

As was mentioned at the beginning of this booklet, many of the problems with religious language are due to the fact that religious language attempts to deal with things that are beyond our experience. It has also been seen that, because of this, some philosophers have felt that religious statements must therefore be meaningless, whereas others have tried to say in what ways it may be possible to talk about religious ideas. However, as a consequence of the work of some philosophers it is possible that the problems of religious language may be dissolved.

Many 20th Century philosophers have argued that religious ideas are in need of reinterpretation. It is argued that religious language should no longer be seen as being about the "transcendent" or the "metaphysical" as really it is about things that we all experience. The "problems" of religious language therefore disappear as religious language is no longer seen to be about things that are beyond experience. What is needed is a removal of the "metaphysical jargon" of religion and religious language should be reduced to a different medium. Indeed what religion is all about, according to some, is not some external being but our own psychology and feelings. This approach has become known as "reductionism".

Perhaps the most influential person who advocated this view was Tillich whose ideas we have already considered. God is, according to Tillich, no longer a "Being" but is "being itself". This idea has been adopted by others such as John Robinson and more recently Don Cupitt. Further, D.Z. Phillips provides a good example of the way in which religious language should be reinterpreted. For Phillips the phrase "eternal life" has nothing to do with living forever, rather it is concerned with our own psychology and the quality of life that we should be experiencing now.

The idea that religion can be reinterpreted has been criticized. Many religious ideas are based on factual claims and if, for example, "God" is no longer to be considered a transcendent being, it is diffi-

cult to see whether religion can any longer be considered signifi-
cant. If religious terms are only about our own psychology, what reason is there to be religious? Take, for instance, the idea of prayer. A
reductionist might say that prayer is about expressing our hopes
and fears about the future. However, it might be argued that this
devalues prayer as people only pray because they believe that their
prayers might come true.

COMMON MISUNDERSTANDINGS

"What is the difference between true and meaningful?"

It is possible to confuse the two terms "true" and "meaningful". However, it is important to remember that when discussing whether a sentence is meaningful we are only interested in whether it makes sense not whether it is actually the case. For example, "all swans are pink" makes sense but is not true.

"Is there a difference between meaning and meaningful?"

Some of the philosophers that have been mentioned attempted to provide a definition of what meaning is. The logical positivists, for example, argued that meaning is the "method of verification". If we can establish what meaning is, we would have a criterion or code by which statements could be judged either meaningful or meaningless. Thus for the logical positivists if something cannot be verified, it cannot have meaning (which is the verification principle). Hence meaningful is concerned with whether a statement makes sense whereas meaning explains what the statement says.

"How does the analytic/synthetic distinction affect religious language?"

Some writers have felt, particularly when discussing logical positivism, that the terms "analytic" and "synthetic" are a useful distinction. An analytic statement is one in which the predicate is contained in the idea or definition of the subject (e.g. all spinsters are unmarried) whereas a synthetic statement is one in which the predicate adds something to the subject (e.g. all spinsters are wise). Clearly this distinction could be used when discussing logical positivism as analytic statements are true by definition (i.e. "meaningful but trivial") whereas synthetic statements would need to be verifiable in order to be meaningful.

"Aren't the verification and falsification principles really two sides of the same coin?"

Both the verification and falsification principles are part of the same

20th century tradition of Empiricism. Indeed the phrase "empirical challenge" is often used to describe the criticisms of religious language made by both principles. Whilst there are differences in approach both principles argue that religious language is meaningless as there is a lack of evidence. The verification principle states there can be no evidence that counts in favour of religious statements whereas the falsification principle states there can be no evidence that counts against religious statements.

WORKSHEET

1. Consider the following:
   A. All swans are white
   B. Sheep people yellow
   C. Scientists study science
   D. Sylvester is a cat
   E. Philosophy is fun
   F. aheui kdien gg
   G. 01100101
   H. The King of France is bald
   J. I drove my car yesterday
   K. Purple dreams sleep furiously

   a) For each of the above say whether it is:
      (i) true, false or you cannot determine
      (ii) meaningful or meaningless

   b) By what criteria did you judge that some statements are meaningless?
      Did it differ for different statements?

   c) Does the fact that there is no King of France affect your answers concerning statement H? If so, in what ways?

---

2. Consider the following:
   A. Scientists study science
   B. Water is a liquid
   C. Worthing is by the sea
   D. Hitler invaded Poland
   E. 2+2=4
   F. All teachers are wise
   G. God is omnipotent
   H. Jesus rose from the dead

   a) For each of the above decide whether it is trivial, meaningful or meaningless according to:
      (i) the strong form of the verification principle
      (ii) the weak form of the verification principle.

   b) Provide your own example(s) of a statement that is meaningful according to the weak form and meaningless according to the strong form.

---

3. Consider the following:
   A. The sunset was like molten gold
   B. Red is John Smith's favourite colour
   C. Today was perfect
   D. This book is red
   E. Christians worship God
   F. The world's a stage
   G God performs miracles
   h. I have a friend no-one else can see.

a) For each of the above say whether it is:
   (i) verifiable
   (ii) falsifiable
   (iii) meaningful

b) What do you think that this says about meaning?

---

4. Flew argued that religious statements died a "death of a thousand qualifications".

   a) Explain what you think that this means.

   b) Consider Flew's parable of the gardener. How does this illustrate the above statement?

   c) Do you think that Flew's idea of falsification is a valid way of determining whether something is meaningful? Justify your answer.

---

5. How far do you think the following solve the problems with religious language:

   (i) symbol
   (ii) analogy
   iii) myth
   (iv) language games?

EXAM QUESTIONS

The reason why most people fail exams at "A" level and above is because they write irrelevant information as opposed to inaccurate information. The plea of examiners is always "answer the question asked." However students often regurgitate answers from questions set during their studies. Such 'model' answers are used irrespective of the slant or emphasis in the exam question.

It is important that answers are planned before embarking on an essay. Not only does this allow a student to arrange material in a logical order but serves as an "early warning system" showing whether they have sufficient knowledge to fully answer the question.

Questions on religious language tend to ask for a critical discussion of one area of religious language. Consider the following example:

Outline and evaluate the challenge to religious language that 20th Century empiricism has made.

INTRODUCTION
define empiricism (knowledge/experience etc.)
highlight key ideas of C20th (language, sense experience etc.)

CHALLENGE
God talk is meaningless
Why? Verification
Falsification

EVALUATION
Is God talk meaningless?
Criticisms of verification and falsification
Are there alternative views of language?

FURTHER READING

It is usually possible to find a chapter on religious language in most introductions to the philosophy of religion. For most of the philosophers that have been discussed in this booklet mention has already been made of their major writings and these would be a worthwhile read. The following is a list of some other books that examine and explain religious language. As the issues of religious language are very wide ranging not all the books will cover every issue.

PHILOSOPHY & THE CHRISTIAN FAITH
by Colin Brown (IVP:1968)
Readability: *** Content: ###
Sets the discussion about religious language into an historical framework.

AN INTRODUCTION TO THE PHILOSOPHY OF RELIGION (New Edition)
by Brian Davies (OUP:1993)
Readability: ** Content: ##
Has expanded on previous edition.

RELIGIOUS LANGUAGE
by Peter Donovan (Sheldon Press: 1976)
Readability: *** Content:###
A popular introduction.

PHILOSOPHY OF RELIGION: Thinking About Faith.
by C. Stephen Evans (IVP:1982)
Readability: *** Content: ##
Concentrates particularly on verification and falsification.

REASON AND RELIGIOUS BELIEF
by Peterson et al. (OUP:1991)
Readability: *** Content: ###
Wide ranging and up to date. Also provides useful study questions.Scholarly comments given in commentary sections.

KEY Readability: * manageable;   ** good;
                              *** very good;   **** excellent;
         Content covered: # adequate;   ## good;
                            ### very good;   #### excellent.

GLOSSARY

Analogy—a comparison that attempts to show how two or more things are similar.

Blik—a word coined by R.M. Hare to mean a way of looking at the world.

Empiricism—a major philosophical movement that argues that knowledge must be based on experience.

Eschatological verification—theory that some religious ideas are verifiable after death (or at the end of time).

Falsification principle—theory that states that sentences are only meaningful if some evidence can count against them.

Language game—a term used by Wittgenstein to refer to any particular context in which language is used.

Logical positivism—20th century philosophical movement that criticized metaphysics and adopted the verification principle.

Model—something that represents something else and helps us understand the original.

Myth—a symbolic story that tries to explain a fundamental issue about the purpose of existence.

Negation—denial of something.

Performative language—term used to refer to language that performs a function (rather than describes).

Reductionism—belief that religious ideas should be reinterpreted so that they are about psychology not metaphysics.

Sign—a way of representing something else.

Symbol—something that represents something else and evokes a new insight.

Verification principle—theory that states that sentences are only meaningful if they can be checked by the senses.